Contents

CLASSIC FESTIVAL SOLOS offer the advancing instrumental soloist an array of materials graded from easy to more challenging. An assortment of musical styles has been included to give variety and to allow an opportunity for the musician to develop interpretive skills.

Jack Lamb, Editor

© 1992 BELWIN-MILLS PUBLISHING CORP.
All Rights Administered by WARNER BROS. PUBLICATIONS U.S. INC.
All Rights Reserved including Public Performance for Profit

RHYTHM OF THE BELLS

FRED HOEY

EL03751

Copyright ©1962 by FIRST DIVISION PUBLISHING CORPORATION
Copyright Assigned 1968 to BELWIN MILLS, c/o CPP/BELWIN, INC., Miami, Florida 33014
International Copyright Secured   Made In U.S.A.   All Rights Reserved

4

DRESS PARADE
(Based On "Stars And Stripes Forever")

JOHN PHILIP SOUSA
Arr. by FRED HOEY

EL03751
Copyright © 1970 by BELWIN MILLS, c/o CPP/BELWIN, INC., Miami, FL 33014
International Copyright Secured   Made In U.S.A.   All Rights Reserved

Trio

Trio

UP BEAT PETE'S SUITE

WALLY BARNETT

I. Jazz Waltz

EL03751

Copyright © 1980 by BELWIN MILLS, c/o CPP/BELWIN, INC., Miami, FL 33014
International Copyright Secured   Made In U.S.A.   All Rights Reserved

II. Snare Drum Alone

III. March

Slow March (♩ = 72-90)

BATTLE HYMN OF THE REPUBLIC

arr. by
SANDY FELDSTEIN

Copyright © 1970 by BELWIN MILLS, c/o CPP/BELWIN, INC., Miami, FL 33014
International Copyright Secured   Made In U.S.A.   All Rights Reserved

THAT'S TOUGH

E.L. MASONER
Eaitea by Wally Barnett

Marchtempo (♩=120)

EL03751

Copyright © 1980 by **BELWIN MILLS**, c/o CPP/BELWIN, INC., Miami, FL 33014
International Copyright Secured   Made In U.S.A.   All Rights Reserved

POPPYCOCK

WALLY BARNETT

EL03751

Copyright © 1980 by BELWIN MILLS, c/o CPP/BELWIN, INC., Miami, FL 33014
International Copyright Secured   Made In U.S.A.   All Rights Reserved

WHODUNIT

WALLY BARNETT

EL03751

Copyright © 1980 by BELWIN MILLS, c/o CPP/BELWIN, INC., Miami, FL 33014
International Copyright Secured   Made In U.S.A.   All Rights Reserved

MARCH FOR A DIFFERENT DRUMMER

WALLY BARNETT

Moderate march tempo (♩=120)

EL03751

Copyright © 1980 by BELWIN MILLS, c/o CPP/BELWIN, INC., Miami, Florida 33014
International Copyright Secured   Made In U.S.A.   All Rights Reserved

24

THE NEW MILITARY

SANDY FELDSTEIN

EL03751   Copyright © 1971 by BELWIN MILLS, c/o CPP/BELWIN, INC., Miami, FL 33014
International Copyright Secured   Made In U.S.A.   All Rights Reserved

rimshot

HUM DRUM

WALLY BARNETT

EL03751

Copyright © 1978 by BELWIN MILLS, c/o CPP/BELWIN, INC., Miami, Florida 33014
International Copyright Secured   Made In U.S.A.   All Rights Reserved

CIRCLING

SANDY FELDSTEIN

Copyright © 1970 by BELWIN MILLS, c/o CPP/BELWIN, INC., Miami, FL 33014
International Copyright Secured   Made In U.S.A.   All Rights Reserved

PICKING UP SIX

SANDY FELDSTEIN

EL03751

Copyright © 1970 by BELWIN MILLS, c/o CPP/BELWIN, INC., Miami, FL 33014
International Copyright Secured   Made In U.S.A.   All Rights Reserved

37

EL03751

ONE AND TWO

SANDY FELDSTEIN

EL03751

Copyright ©1971 by BELWIN MILLS, c/o CPP/BELWIN, INC., Miami, FL 33014
International Copyright Secured   Made In U.S.A.   All Rights Reserved